POEMS FOR THE LOST DEER

Copyright © 2014 All rights reserved

Cover painting by Robin H. Lysne
acrylic on canvas
copyright 2012 all rights reserved

ISBN: 978-0-9778645-4-6
Library of Congress number: 2014901714

Poems for the Lost Deer

Published by:
(A cooperative poetry press)
Blue Bone Books
P.O.Box 2250
Santa Cruz, CA

Robin H. Lysne, M.F.A., Ph.D.

rhlysne@cruzio.com
BlueBoneBooks.com
thecenterforthesoul.com

Dedicated to the Deerpeople
and those who love them.

Note to Reader

The following poems have been largely taken from facts about an incident that occurred in 2007 and 2008, and began many years before. In the 1920's the San Francisco Zoo brought Axis deer (from the Ceylon Islands, East India) and Fallow deer (from Mediterranean, Persia and Eurasia) to San Francisco. In 1947-49 they sold their over-populations to Dr. Millard Ottinger, a rancher who owned a large track of land on Pt.Reyes peninsula in Marin County, California just north of San Francisco.

Some of these poems are from found language from actual articles written over a period of thirty years from 1974 until 2008. Some documentation comes from National Park Service (NPS) website, including the Pt. Reyes National Seashore website and from the White Buffalo, Inc. website listed in the back on the List of Sources page.

References to Native American language and culture are not intended appropriations of language or culture, but come authentically from my experience of the last thirty years with various tribal groups who have generously taught me some of their language, allowed me to dance in their sacred dances, and who have shared with me the values, that they knew I also shared with them. If there are any errors in these references they are my own. All tribal references other than Lakota, have been found in books, or on websites and are replicated commonly, and all references are noted in the back of the book in the end pages.

My intention in this book is to honor those who fought, raised awareness, and loved the deer. The balance of the voices heard in these pages is about the percentage of the people for and against the deer in the story. I hope in some small way, it questions the policies of invasive species created by the National Park Service. But most of all, I wish to honor the magical deer that lived in Pt. Reyes before the National Seashore was even developed as a national park.

The following poems have been previously published:

"Writing without Walls", on-line reading and print journal February, 2012:
    "Don't shoot I'm white and non-native"
    Expedition
    Lost Deer revised from publication

Samizdat Literary Journal On-line and print journal January, 2010
    Shoulder Blade" drawing/poem

Table of Contents

Copyright page..ii
Dedcation..iii
Note to the Reader..ix
Table Of Contents...vi

Point Reyes..1
Anthony Godola Remembers..3
I tucked a tuft..5
Deerise...6
Across the Field..8
If we are to make a more perfect union..9
Headlines: Rangers..10
We have been roaming..11
Even then she watched...12
From here...13
1985 Trailside Guide...14
Facts about Deer..15
Word Arrows...16
Hunter Dream..17
Dreamvision..18
Question #1 For the Park Ranger...19
Earth Sent Us..20
Take Care Sleeping Fawn...21
Picture-poem Sleeping Fawn..24
Omen...25
Parks wants to get rid...26
An Occult Balance..27
Expedition...28
Question #2 for the Park Ranger..30
Fans of Buckhorn..31
Questions #1 for the Shooter..32
The Politics of Shooting Deer..34
Grandfather Fire asks..35
The Gentle Wild is Leaving..36
Sisters and Brothers please...37
Somewhat Logically...38
Dear Editor..39
Seven Upon Seven..40
Two Extremes...42

Woman and a White Unicorn	44
Picture-Poem-Woman Deer	45
All my armor	46
Don't shoot	47
Lost	48
Out here	49
You can lay the Death	50
Question # 3 for the Park Ranger	51
Down there Comes a Fallow Doe	52
Humans raise their long reeds	53
Who is Not an Invasive Species	54
Language Lessons	55
Humans came	56
They herd together	57
Picture Poem-Deer Herd with Tags	58
Big Red Tags	59
January 31, 2008	60
Pt. Reyes Earth Voice	61
Deer Carcases	62
No Middle Way	63
Afterwards	64
Photo of the Wailing Wall	64
Question #2 for the Shooter	64
What I want to Say to You	66
Picture-Poem-Deer Eating with Tree	67
To find our lost Deer	68
Gentle Deer	69
Deer Say	70
What These Deer Mean	71
Earth is So Damaged	72
Picture-Poem-Single Deer Grazing from Branches	73
Earth to Humans	74
She Called Herself Black Hair Sild Girl Wind	75
Picture-Poem-Piebald Deer	76
Cullng Continues	77
Everything without tags and a Collar	78
Gone-a-Con Blues	79
Plan #1 and Plan #2	81

After the kill..82
The Search..83
Picture-Poem-Shoulder Blade..87
Bright Sightings..88
Picture-Poem-Dream for Deer..90
Dream fot the Deer...91
Death of the Wild...92
Along Mountain base...93
After the massacre..94
The Deer on this Canvase...95
Lament for the DeerPeople...96
Full Moon Clock Tower..97
Acknowledgements...98
List of Sources..100
About the Author..101

POEMS FOR THE LOST DEER

by

Robin White Turtle Lysne

Point Reyes,

an odd island spoking its way

up the coast a few inches a year,

splitting down the middle Tomales Bay

that wide blue thumb of salt water,

resting uneasy on the Pacific Plate

the other bayside the North American Plate

this triangle of wild green slides daily,

jumped in one jolt twenty feet northwest

in 1906.

It is brown all summer,

except in the fog line where it's green all year.

90,000 acres of the seashore

sea lions and seals on the beaches

tidal pools house starfish and mussels, crabs where

shale shingles down

cliffs. From the shore rolling hills,

creeks through deep Bay Laurel forests

or Monterey Pine so thick the butterflies

graveyards hang above in spectrum of orange and black

to shaded grays. Corpses in layers from high trees die

after mating in dark blue thickets to hide

deer, raccoons, possums in Cyprus

Redwood groves, pockets where
trees end the glades begin
meadows and fields full of Tule Elk,
black-tailed deer abundant
this is where you see them on the edge
of green through thickets
folding over the land, a river of palmate antlers
brown and white beards of Axis deer, black paired with
white fawn spots on grown adults of Fallow deer.
Mountain lions tracks over owls pellets near mouse holes
and Red-Tail hawks circling wherever you look up.
This is the wild preserved, un-manicured
the way it was, is, would be without
modern humans multiplying. The Miwoks
lived here without much change
for thousands of years. Since 1972
Pt. Reyes National Seashore became
a national park, a sanctuary,
charged with protecting these wild lands
forever.

Anthony Gondola Remembers

*"I was hired to pick up Doc Ottinger's deer from the Zoo
in 1949.*
                            In the photograph Mr. Gondola's face

                                          was rippled brown furrows.
He was a good Doctor, he liked to hunt.
                  His hands could receive a baby, yet were creased
           with dirt from moving bricks and soil on his small farm.
Doc had white deer and black deer on his ranch
in Olema. Olema flat used to be a green field
cattle, deer grazed together.
                  Behind him, his garden, full of statuary
                  a white deer next to a miniature windmill,
            crushed stones making paths around fruit trees.
That was before the Park changed the course of the creek,
  now there is nothing.   Beyond his garden   golden rolling hills,
                         Cyprus and Redwood in patches.
White deer were seen when we went to church.
    You've got the park here and the recreation area
                    white pickets of his yard
              shared with his wife   contain their world
They did away with all the farmers.
                  All that farmland is going to waste.

Those animals

        The deer with them as newlywed, thirty-years before the

                  park started

should have a right to roam all over. "[1]

---

1. Interview with Ambrose Gondola, PT Reyes Light, May 8, 2008

I tucked a tuft into my hat.
Laying down strands of hair in exchange

An old Indian song rose up in my throat:

Pelamayeo,   Palamayeo
Thank you, Thank you Creator,
Wakan Taka, Toka Heya, Che wa kealo.

Tufts of their fur lay at my feet.
seven white deer appear
grazing on a hillside

an apparition? Their presence answers
their gaze at me, going back to grazing,
just after asking for a sign

Is writing my path?

After fasting for two days, walking those hills
Rounding the corner of a yellow trail…

Deerise

Four a.m.
        snow-covered Michigan morning
            sauna steam
    releases all scent
        from my body
            keeps me warm
at my birth time the 3rd day of January, my 33rd year.

I walk out into snow covered woods
        as a purple shadow
            as a long moon lit trail
                bare trees arch over
                      shadow fingers interlock

Wearing a lightning bolt blanket
        crocheted by my grandmother
            smelling cold winter clear
                her arms still around me in her labor
I sit at the end of the road… in a crossroads

Moon a bright disk
    steam rises
        laying my coat down under me   boots on
            settling in   sitting for my dive into self
    a soft gaze out sitting in shadow   waiting
            waiting   listening to night
                an hour passes
                    then a stirring near by
    three deer rise behind me
        sleepy   waking slow
            legs close enough to touch
                to smell their musty fur
they saunter down the same trail I had come up
        a four point rack buds on one in silhouette
            with the dawn sun
                only a blue glow on one horizon lip

a threesome
        become shadow
                a wild must
                        gait along
        saunter down
                a moon-blue trail
trees arching
        over

                I rise

Across this
field an apple tree
full of blossoms
run to it, sniff
stretching our necks
rub antlers on bark
scratch ears with hooves,
nuzzle young
we live
one more
spring.

If we are to make a more perfect union, we the people of the United States, especially of the dominant culture, need strive for less perfection, might try disobedience, we did it in in the 60s. If we want to have dominion, which we interpret as domination, perhaps we need to walk the fields first. Turn off those cell phones, which lord over us, and not forget about stewardship, or embeddedness, as man is simply not above nature in any way, except our gray matter which we misuse continually to justify atrocities. If we truly would listen to what god, a god like us, could do, we would leave them be, and not manage species, control populations, pretend to be the deciders. What we have done, label them "invasives" then find evidence against them, we 'other,' then invent, 'other' then condemn, we have done this from our roots, our European heritage from the witch burnings, there and here, to the Native American genocide, to making the African people slaves, to the Nazi justification to exterminating the Jews, to the Tuskegee experiments, and now, shifting our focus, to the creatures, we manage these deer populations. Why? Why must we "other" then invent, condemn, silence, then exterminate? Same old story. On infinitum, eternityum. We continue the way our fathers did, and perhaps that is the problem. Let's follow our mothers or find a new way, follow The Mother, how she provides and cares for us for all creatures equally. The native people had it right. Respect this Earth Mother, Sky Father, sit together in a circle. Perhaps sustainability could be in our gray matter. For if we are the royal-we, when we focus on the deer, that have not harmed, though there are those who would say, let's see, the argument, yes, they harm the native deer, push them out, drive them out, Did they really? No, all evidence shows they do not, they do not eat the same thing, they do not interbreed, they mingle but graze in peace even with cattle and sheep. Oh say can you see did I say too many, that these foreign invasives, aliens, these exotics, and those lek sites-where male deer rut-make holes that disturb the landscape, do you know they grow over and over, so *why* do we other, puritanically, and other, forever and ever amen?

WethePeopleinordertomakeamore perfectUnion havetomakethings perfecthavetorecognizeourpower, wehavetoseethatwearethepeople wearethepeopleWethePeople in ordertomakeamoreperfectUnion havetomakethingsperfecthaveto recognizeourpower,wehavetosee thatwearethepeoplewearethe peopleWethePeopleinordertomake amoreperfectUnionhavetomake thingsperfecthavetorecognizeour power,wehavetoseethatwearethe peoplewearethepeopleWethePeople inordertomakeamoreperfectUnion havetomakethingsperfecthaveto recognizeourpower,wehavetosee thatwearethepeoplewearethepeop

Headlines: Rangers hunt deer in National Seashore not hunters as decided in community meetings.

Things are different here. Since the 40's community waits on decisions. 22 exotics, North Indian fallow deer, their herds flowing over, inspire peace look so grace-filled on our green hills. Giant Bambis come to stasis. They don't push out black-tailed deer, they just eat more silverspot, bark from trees in lean times.

Things are different here. Don't shoot in my backyard—stop killing! Public demands. Outrage in the 70's 400-700 roam, graze, rut, mate, yet 400-800 Iraqi deer too many. Things are different here. Things are different here! Rangers cull not hunt in season after fog embedded park policy. As long as we eliminate roaming we promote, what ideal, our jobs as keepers? Park says: Seasonal estimates different here. In the 80's NPS policy says: We must eliminate non-natives but things different here, white fallow deer in India, holy, roam, graze, rut, mate. This is Marin County, things are different here, wait things are different here. Institution kills not blood thirsty hunters, citizens and park agrees, and things are different, here. Wait. This is how things are
...

10

We
have been
roaming these green
hills as long as any of us
remember. How many
generations of deerpeople
must be born before all
beings know we
belong here?

Even then, she watched, then released,
watched and released turtles, guppies, worms, foals, fawns.
Deer raced through the pines at night.

We put the turtle in the kitchen sink
with paint on its cheeks, learned its name,
then put it back in the Great Lake.

How the sisters played in the dunes
and waited for adults to go in
so we could swim.

We saw turtles in the water then, minnows, spiders
walking on water. "Jesus spiders" Grandpa would chuckle.
Swimming in it, *Are there fishes?*
Do they bite toes?

She listens to the rush of
water on sand. Thoughts between laps
wondering about this broad water, where does it go?

A four-year old girl surveys sand dunes, this broad water,
a corn cob pipe in her mouth,
her Bambi sunglasses on.

        From here
a green lawn in two shades

           Sun on half
    dark green shadow from
redwood tree shading here.

      Thunderheads dark gray
         send wind to turn
        leaves inside out.
                  Line between greens

                      erased

                            wind picks up

             sun is hidden   suddenly.

           Stretchingoutwinds
               blow
                     flags straight.
          Willowsnotweeping

                            anymore.

1985
Trailside Guide

Deer of Pt. Reyes National Seashore

Several wild and reproducing species
Intermingle while grazing, but do not interbreed.
CONTROL
They live in boundaries, all 71,000 acres, or
100 square miles of the Point Reyes National Seashore.
CONTROL
Black-tailed deer (Odocoileus hemionus columbianus) Do not form
herds. They do not migrate but live in the same area their entire lives.
CONTROL
Eight exotic Axis (axis axis) or chital (white spotted) deer from
India, Ceylon were brought here by a SF. Doctor in 1947 and 8.
CONTROL
Today there are four and five hundred.
CONTROL
Fallow (dama dama) come
from Mediterranean to Asia Minor
CONTROL
brought here by the same doctor he brought
28 from San Francisco Zoo in 1949.
CONTROL
Englishmen kept semi-domesticated deer in parks
Where selective breeding has produced
CONTROL
Numerous coat colorings. George Washington brought
Fallow deer. In America, they come from English stock.
CONTROL
Bucks have large palmate antlers like a moose
October rut bucks and does come together in large herds
CONTROL
Antlers shed in April. Fawns born in mid-June, rarely occurring as
twins fawns are often different colors than mother.
CONTROL
Recent studies show that if the populations are unchecked numbers

will compete for forage with native black-tailed deer and livestock.
CONTROL
PRNS is initiating a program of exotic deer management, which consists of continued research to determine optimum population levels.
CONTROL
We monitor deer reduction keep the population within these limits. Exotic deer are controlled by selective shooting employed by park personal.
CONTROL
Proper deer management will assure a smaller population of healthy deer instead of a larger number of deer in poor physical condition.

Facts about the Mesopotamian Fallow Deer

The Persian Fallow Deer (Dama mesopotamica) is a ruminant mammal belonging to the family Cervidae.
ABSTRACT: The Persian fallow deer Dama dama mesopotamica is extremely rare in the wild, but reintroduction of breeding animals from the Hai-Bar Carmel, Israel, may be feasible. The Persian fallow deer (Dama dama mesopotamica) is classified as Endangered, but other subspecies are not considered to be at threat.
The Persian subspecies (Dama dama mesopotamica) is 20-25% larger.
The Mesopotamian or Persian fallow deer(Dama dama mesopotamica) is considered to be one of the rarest species of deer in the world; overhunting brought this species to the verge of extinction worldwide.

Mesopotamia -- (the land between the Tigris and Euphrates; site of several ancient civilizations) Mesopotamia
2. Source WordNet

Word

arrows

struck

spun me around

Those deer

Exterminated?

They were a great sign
once,

pointing toward a life direction

as the heron this evening

circles around   landing   in the west

in the old Eucalyptus

arched   confident wings
spread wide.

Now the bird   is   a   sign   rising,

Though the deer are gone,

still forever   embedded

into   Earth's   nervous   system

as the Great Blue

knows–is telling

cannot comprehend

what humans do.

Hunter Dream

Walking up the hill from a dark road
Orion is shooting arrows into my house
Lights are on   so he has hit his target.

No one else is home.

His fiery body sending arrows
without poison tips, but with love tips
this time,

Has the hunter found his Juréma?
Entering the house
seven white deer are grazing
silent in the darkness.

Dreamvision

Born to Earth
she flew up and out of it
towards me
shrieking her wild cry
her fist holding an
obsidian blade
plunging into flesh
from pubic bone to throat
splits me open
rivers and streams, forests
alive with
rocks and snails follow

She was not through
she came again and this time
I was unafraid
I opened my arms
wider this time
still and again she lunged
and again
more trees and forests
and laughter pours
from creeks where wild salmon
swim up

a third time she flies
screaming wild uvular
vocables
and this time
plunges
her black blade
deeper still
and I surrender into
rocks and rivulets
pouring out
around
ever since.

Question #1 for a Park Ranger:

How are species managed?

Pick a date, draw a line.

Whatever team of experts deem—

this is the way it is.

What species are non-native?

Pick a date, any date—

300 years ago? 150? Why not 75?

Just draw (bleep'n) a line.

Earth sent us.
We came as sign
singing in rivers
over green hills
running wild.

Take care
       sleeping fawn

How do we   stop them
from (k)culling   you?

Lenape, Ohlone, Chumash, Yokut, Salinan

If I sing
will you hear me
in your sleep?

Time to wake up
wake up
see writing
on the tree
behind you

Lenape, Ohlone, Chumash, Yokut, Salinan

Protestors tried
still continue
chest hurts
with the killing

forest child
sleeping fawn
wake up
wake up

 Protests didn't do it
or did they save a few?
stop it…

enough…

this chest hurts
with killing

tree child

all of us

Perhaps hunters
didn't know
these truths
from so many
different tribes:

Lenape, Ohlone, Chumash, Yokut, Salinan

The Lenape say:

a pair
of white deer
       is peace
                      abundance
for everyone

The presence
of a white deer

      teaches respect   for all life

Celts say white deer are
        messengers from
               the other world

      A white deer companions the god Fukurokuju in Japan

Hungarians and Lenape say: spotted white deer
      walk between worlds
are a message from the Great Spirit

taking a white deer
        shortens one's life

Seneca say: to kill a white deer
        keeps one in this world
no bridge over

Seneca, Roanoke Algonquin, Nanticoke, Pocomoke,
Lenape, Ohlone, Chumash, Yokut, Salinan

what was done to
300 native tongues

was done to people
who spoke them
a few remain
a few still survive… wake up
sleeping fawn
run!

Lenape, Ohlone, Chumash, Yokut, Salinan

Take care of this sleeping fawn. How do we stop things from eating you? How can we protect you. It's scary to your mom. How to protect what is sacred? How do we help the fellings? Protects debt love. Maybe you can operate to no. Protection is out - why should we have to protect. Don't people get it? Did you know how precious life is? What are these children of the trees are here for all of us. Why that we stop leaving our places. Quie else is it of what there is going to brake out into a new world that we already know.

Even though a drawing, this is not bambi it has flesh and bones. You are so loved, so loved, so loved - you are so loved. Even as a ghost, ghostly deer we love you. You are so loved.

So much on this sleeping back though it carries what it carries lightly sleeping baby wake up and run time to get up + move it.

To kill a white deer shortens one's life, according to the Lenape people. To see a pair together is a sign of ever lasting peace and prosperity for all the peoples. To see a spotted white deer is to see one who walks between worlds. All this according to lenape. To kill a spotted white deer is to keep one person in one world, no bridge over.

This deer may not see adult hoods or meals or find its spots hopping along in the grass - time to get up to wake up time is now.

Omen

Gazalles stabbed by hunters become Ghazels, so stand in the rain.
Fallow deer lay fallow by sides of roads and stand in the rain.

Axis bunch together cry a sharp yowp,
Culling means slaughter as hunters take aim and stand in the rain.

Seven white deer slain as the wrong species
Protestors bring petitions, hold hands, signs and stand in the rain.

When you spoke I spun as if you shot me
When you told me of this omen I watched you stand in the rain.

for Agha Shahid Ali

Park wants to get rid

of Un-American Deer.

'To choose who may

live and who may not

is a flawed ideology

for controlling nature,

an unexamined

Judeo-Christian attitude

dating from the book

of Genesis.'[1]

Dominus,
dominion (noun)
don-min-ions
1.ruling control
2..shere of influence
3..land ruled
4. self-governing territory
5.L domus = house dominus a lord
6. dominion
7. domnaion femninin,
8.maitrise feminine;
9.terrritoire masculine
10.dominion masculine
11.

[3]. Point Reyes Light, February 10th, 2005, found language poem quoting Ilka Hartman of Bolinas, CA

An Occult Balance

in my backyard as[1]

                          gunshots disrupted
                                    meditators.
                    Sheriffs say nothing
          to worry about, just the culling.
                              Caller knew about the culling
                    wanted to be sure

nothing
                                        was wrong.
            Though they forbade killing on
                            their land,
         Though the teachings of Vedanta
                      see all life sacred
                   Vedanta Retreat Center is
open to all
impose no moral stance.
"Each person has to find
          their own moral path"
They neither support nor
          oppose the culling.
     "We don't support this type of thing
                we do live in the world and are part of it."

---

4. Pt. Reyes Light, January 31, 2008, article by Tess Elliot

Expedition

No white deer rolling over

green rainy hills were seen

But there were

four black ravens

careening up one side of the road

to the other then down again

A herd of Tule Elk walking across the road in front

of my car, too may to count at first

then around the green grass glades

and ocean falling away below

more elk, a group running down the hillside

over open range

No rare sacred white deer on the hillsides

though chanted songs for a vision were sung,

put out tobacco prayers from inside this car window

But there were giant puff balls on the ridge coming back

and a heard of black and white Holsteins

running towards the fence, a group of Angus across the road.

There was that long view over Tomales Bay up on the ridge, and

Limantour beach stretching out and out along the

curve of Pt. Reyes shore, and white rocks that could have been them

could have been but wasn't

Then a lift of birds soaring in the rain wheeling around in the stiff wind

Vision Road was closed and Hearts Desire Beach gated

but then a dozen trees covered with Spanish moss dripped wet

the sweetness of fresh wind off the ocean

and no deer

rain misting

then pouring down relentless.

Question #2 for a Park Ranger:

What are the management factions?

            Did I say all management is political?

    Scientist Say: Our Data shows

        we need so much water for

        logging

        fisheries

        wildlife,   Politicians say:

                      We need to cut trees for

                          jobs

        houses,   imports

So they take 100 feet along streams and rivers.

                      Do they really need that much land?

        Loggers just take anyway

        Fines not big enough to

                offset trees.   Ranchers say: Don't

let the wolves,   bears,   mountain lions

                                      kill my

                              cows, pigs, sheep

Then there are the tourists.

Just passing through, with boats, RV's, trailers.

Did I say all management is political? Did I say I protect the park from people?

People from people?

           Fans of
          buckhorns
        rise like black
        palms startled
           in our
           grazing

              rain

   shots
 pop across
   fields

            watch

                    our
                   fallen
                 blood mix
                 with wet
                   grain.

Question #1 for the Shooter
Could you talk about your work?

I love the environment, technology, projects.
Put that all together that is what I do.

We do the best we can to remove them lethally.
It's a niche I fell into. You can't think about the
individual animal you have to think about them
as a species. We eradicate invasive species.
You have to be meticulous.

In the long run,
does anything
we do matter?
Probably not.

I keep defining
methods,
perfecting them.
I make my own
darts for
sterilizations.

Managing deer is
more rewarding as
people have disrupted
their habitat,
just like the Native Americans—
you want that space?
We eradicate them too—
It is the same thing as killing the deer.
It is our way to limit their use
so we can keep propagating.

All management is because of
human overpopulation.
But no one wants to address that.

Whether you kill things intentionally
things die because you live.
Whether you live in a house,
drive a car, or go to work
you are killing things
every day. People aren't
comfortable with their own
predation.

The Politics of Shooting Deer

St Anthony's shelter

receives butchered carcasses

dressed down in farm dining room

hunting occurs at dawn

morning dreams become nightmares.[5]

---

5. Point Reyes Light, April 7, 2005, Inspired by an article by John Hulls

Grandfather Fire asks

to gather wood at the fence

of your longing

walk

into the woods

build a pit, fire, sit

around this old voice

talk to me,

my flames

sing

listen

embers

burn

away

your

fears.

The gentle wild is leaving,
No shelters for those who
crave generosity, community, living within
forests, near streams embedded in wild places

        These tired instruments of destruction and imbalance,
Greed, domination, fear, anger, control, overpopulation of humans,
                aggression, erroneous beliefs, lack,

                      hold us back.

Recover
what touches, caresses, embraces,
wild acres
watch deer rise
sun rise,
sleep in hollows as trails wind through
at dusk.

Sisters and Brothers   please   must we say this?

    We
        cannot afford to be against

        nature in any way
                any more.

Must we say this?

We are nature   herself.

    So much broader   than   mind

Giant Oceanic Heart 10,000 times more intelligent.

We   have   scientifically   i=n=t=e=l=l=e=c=t=u=a=l=i=z=e=d
        our   selves and everything else   to   death.

We are dominant.   Yes. predators, yes.

    But   we   have choice   we might just surrender to
what is   as
    water,   earth   air   fire   join,

                become.

    And   those dear

        deer   who   never
harmed
        any

one.
Must we say this?

They have a right to exist too.

Somewhat Logically

I feel therefore…

Take a stand, make it clear to us, NPS

Stand in the Age of Reason

Show us clear evidence

show us reasons *not* to

exterminate

eliminate

evict

you!

You say

whosoever disagrees

with our ironclad overwhelming research

with the voice of this ultra-logical dissemination

of overwhelming foreign invasives, exotics overrunning us

Foreign elements do not make for a more perfect union threaten this

dominant species

The face of our white papers of our need for usefulness how the meek

shall laydown

for us again, and again so we might prove our superiority how these

banners wave

and wag and wave on and on and on. [1]

5. Point Reyes Light, April 7, 2005, Inspired by an article by John Hulls

Dear Editor,

Help!

A spreading stain of violence

against wild things

and us

in our park.

Isn't it our park?[1]

6. Pt. Reyes Light, May 15, 2005, Mardi Woods, Bolinas, CA

Seven Upon Seven
In honor of Agha Shahid Ali and his Ghazals

Seven White Gazelles roamed the hills and came to a spring.
No fear, only drinking the clear waters as they drank from the spring.

Before the seven deer came, footsteps were scoured into the earth of the beloved. Before the beloved one was slaughtered, his love tears came from the spring.

Before the beloved deer came to drink without fear, a grandchild was killed for no reason, out of rage out of fear and two sides are formed, and tears with fear fell into the spring.

Writers launched stories from the poets who came to see the deer without fear, and find their beloved, as they roamed the hills as omens to poets who came to the spring.

And soon others came to see the deer that came to the spring. They brought their beliefs and argued over the meaning of the grandson's death, as they drank from the spring.

Soon the writers and artists came to heal others of their fear who came to see deer, and soon the poets and doctors came and the doctors drank from the spring.

Before you know it lawyers and doctors and judges came to the spring But they came with fear, wanted to know the facts. Then someone said, near the spring,

But these deer are not indigenous and people argued about it and soon someone said they must go. The split ripped apart the fabric of everything as they drank from the spring.

So lawyers and judges shot them and Seven White Gazelles
drank as ghosts from the spring.

Seven artists drank from the spring, and said, *but we are not indigenous either!* Seven upon seven came to the spring bathing and crying and dying at the spring and the waters were poisoned now with more fear. The blood of artists, poets, deer, lawyers, doctors, judges, could not drink, did not see Gazelles, as they wept by the spring,

Said the people lied as they told stories that were myths could not figure out why they had been shot nor who shot them or if it was true as they poisoned the spring.

And soon, the artists and writers became judges and lawyers
And the spring retreated into the Earth. There were no more springs.

No more stories. And the judges and lawyers, artists and poets died and all their ghosts came to the hole in the earth where once was a spring.

They wept for the spring and the deer and the truth that once there was no fear where the beloved walked that day, mourning the tear in the fabric of all things beginning at the spring.

Longing for a new story to be told, ghost deer and poets who found their beloveds, roam and come to drink now in a new land at the edge of a clear spring.

(Preferred reading by two people)

Two

No killing
No hunting
No death
No killing

No hunting wrong

Wrong its wrong wrong
No death
No pain
No suffering

Guns? No killing   no hunting   animals those peaceful   deer
Who are we?   Guns and Uniforms?

No killing
Uniforms
no blood
thirsty   Hunters like it
No death
No killing
No   no! Creating good
Destroying
No destroying
suffering   no death

Blood-thirsty hunter!
No I don't
Cause no   no causing harm!

No no, no
killing

Yes   Life, Peace, silence!
Silence is peace
You wouldn't understand.
No No Death
Life   Life!
No killing !

Extremes

Yes kill
Yes hunt
Death is
Kill
Shoot to kill
Yes
                 hunting is good
Death   feeds

Kill.   Death Is.
        Part of
survival
Who   we   are.
Kill with guns and uniforms. War is
       justified
We   are   killers
Animals
Who is above death?
Justified   Who   who
who is above eating
tasting the kill?
No creation
with out destroying
You kill plants,
chickens, why not
deer, cows, pigs
You kill
Everyday   No death?
No hunting, no eating?
Who is above suffering ?
Silence is death
Who is above death?
      You beyond death?
Death brings life
Death feed life.
No life without it.

No kidding.

Woman and a white unicorn
sit inside a wide picket fence,
a million flowers blooming
a lion on her right
unicorn on the left
a mirror
reflecting
this beast
in her hand
she is well contained
within a white picket fence.

White deer, white unicorn, horses
dolphins, beasts,
ancient symbols
of   chastity, purity, magic,

A Celtic communication, Arthurian legend
creativity unfettered inside,
though thought, desire,
a constant longing
for something beyond
the fence. Free as the wild deer.

Walking
along a trail out beyond the gate
her answer
answers back
reverberating
through the mirror she walks into, beyond
this woman
and the Unicorn, deer, white brown, black, red
a color of the four directions,
rare, unfettered beasts and
a woman
in her power
as herself.

No one can destroy me this time.[1]

[7]. Inspired by the six tapestries, Museum of the Renaissance, Paris, France

All my armor |\ /| has been dissolved
My shields ⬭ are down

There are no slings (nor rocks *
*
nor bows) nor arrows \/\/
\/\/
… no bullets …can penetrate
my spirit ~~~
~~~

•   there are no weapons •-
•-   …
no swords no arrows
 no arrows that will harm me
my heart ♥dear heart ♠
♠
intact ¤✡🛡∞ ☺ ☼•
¤✡🛡∞ ☺ ☼•
and no-thing
will penetrate sing to river ~~~wood |^|^|^|^|^|
~~~|^|^|^|^|^|

You might kill this body ♀♂
but my spirit lives ☼
long after
the hunt >>>>
My spirit is invincible ∞
nothing can harm this beast! ☺

Sing to the moon! ●   (
 She pours
down
light ||||||||||
relentlessly
If you listen the hills ~~sing
with the memory☼•
of our hooves ^^^^^
our cry~~~ ~~ ~~~

Don't shoot-I'm white and non-native

                                        We value dynamic conversations that

                                                          enhance

                                                public engagement.

Baited feeding stations for does-shot 5 to 1

over male deer. Does never return to their young hiding in grasses.

      Civic engagement builds sustained relationships that are necessary for

                              NPS for conservation, stewardship over the long term.

Fawns slowly starve to death.

                                Civic engagement encompasses a set of

                                          diverse techniques

Bodies found by citizens found wounds to the abdomen.

                                  and mutually beneficial relationships.

Buffalo sharp-shooters supposedly were hired to make a

single lethal shot to the head and neck.

    In recent years various activities have led to a deeper reflection on the

                                      importance of civic engagement.

8. Point Reyes Protest - National Park Service Headquarters – 2008, found language poem. Left side Italics: *S.F. Chronicle*, *January 2008*. Right side without Italics: NPS Website, 2011

Lost   up

deer

mean   away

lost

us.

Side

wise

pops   Citizens

                                                                   cry

slam   out,

against

                                                                listen

Wide   to

veils   ghastly

of   echoes…

screams

white

ghosts

float

Out here

my deer are somewhere
on this spit launching out

Rain did not stop me
just being in the wild is enough

Fur of the Tule Elk puff
tufts on their hides molting

A sign, *No Gathering Antlers*
from this Tule Elk Preserve

A clear invitation and no one to stop me
from looking for my Heart's Desire

out near a frigid ocean where
wind blasts horizontal

"You can lay the death
of the white deer,
the Axis and Fallow deer,
squarely at the feet
of the Superintendent
of Point Reyes
National Seashore."[1]

                      Deer comments
                      due by Friday

                      Plan for the deer is
                      not short sighted

                      Exotic Deer trashing
                      our ecosystem

                      Surplus Zoo Animals
                      must be removed

                      Proposed plan of elimination
                      is sound and humane

                      The longer we wait
                      the more biological damage

                      and the more costly
                      lets not forget,
                      costly.[2]

---

9. David Mitchell, former editor of Pt. Reyes Light. At a dinner with protestors, January, 2012
10. Pt. Reyes Light, April 7, 2005, Guest Column

Question #3 for a Park Ranger:
How are plans developed?

Management plans
typically
include a three
or four prong approach
Culling
Education
Garbage cans
stuff like that.

I just work in an office somewhere.
The one with the initiative
takes on the projects
to get promotions

I just want to keep my job.

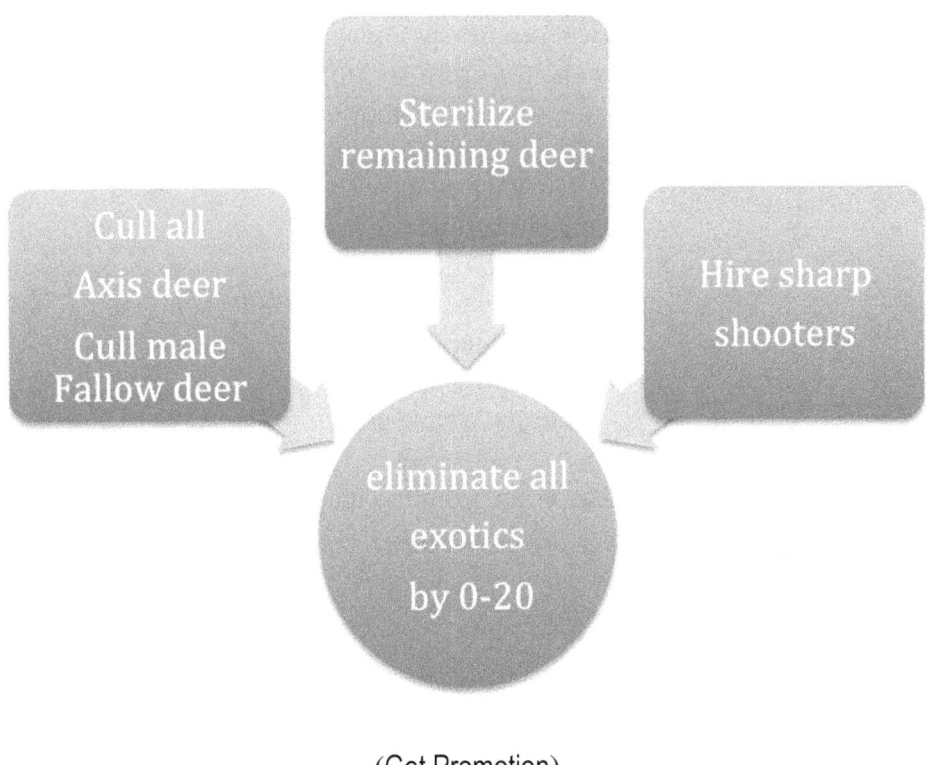

(Get Promotion)

Down there comes a fallow Doe
As great with young as she might goe[1]

We do not need to speak often
to each other –
a lift of head
twist of ear
tells us.

Earth
drums into
our hooves
we spring
up darting
every which way
for cover.

Great birds
Beat air
Beat our thirsty tounges
for shelter, crow says to us
run, run, they come, they come!

We run out
from behind trees
startled

No where to go
signaling to each
other we weave grass

They come from too many
directions

Humans raise long reeds
aim

deer fall into ditch everywhere
no relief mothers fathers brothers
all the brothers
fall
all mothers
shot with needles
no young to nurse
in spring.

---

11. From 16th Century English Ballad, Three Ravens, this metaphoric reference relates the Fallow deer to a woman.

Who is Not an Invasive Species?

Brought to the Zoo from Persia from the Zoo to a rancher
who bought them to hunt, they got loose, have been roaming the hills
since 1948 as

                                                                               an invasive species

Then why are we hunting them now when
they are protected where they came from? They are an endangered species

Fallow Deer and Axis Deer used to roam hills of Persia
only a few left there, 45-65 in the wilds of Iraq, Iran an

                                                                             endangered species

the rest in captivity. Here they are
called invasive species. They have been thriving here as

                                                                               invasive species

Axis and Fallow deer brought to Point Reyes
Then why is the Seashore Superintendent   killing them? They are
                                                                             invasive species

Not culling the heard but shooting them
putting plastic bags around their heads. Suffocating them to death.
                                                                             We are invasive species.

Some say they are signs from the Universe, they were for me, mystical a
apparition years ago walking and fasting. Walking, fasting for two days

                                                                       Who are invasive species?

If they are gone, how do they come to show us
what we need to know?
                                                                       We are an endangered species.

If they are gone, how do other budding artists
Find their way, another

                                                                          endangered species.

Recent sightings say there are a few females left to die a
sterile, natural death in the next ten years.
                                                                      We are an invasive species.

But how lonely they are, must be, without their mates,
having watched them all die.
                                                                      Who is the invasive species?

Language Lessons
For my La*kota elders*

Yucicupi, to grasp and take hold,
of our lives, our people, our land, what we are losing

Yucicupi our core, our families, take responsibility
share the burden of survival, live together in harmony.

Wasicu Those who take.
Perhaps it is a sign of our demise
sacred deer murdered
by men who do not care, who are charged with caring.

Tunkasheila
Grandfather
It is a sign for the deer nation
to rise up, take hold, yucicupi, for what we know.

Maka, Unchi
Mother Earth
It is sign, it is a sign, to wake up, wake up,
please wake up, before it is too late.

Cheki iyo, Cheki iyo
Pray for us, pray for us

Humans came
to stop the
hunters

They gave us
three more moons
before the massacre.

They herd together
        used tracking collars
to find
and kill the does

They herd together
        used collars for cattle
Too big, chafe
cause more suffering

They herd together
instead of just marking the sterilized deer
how could they
how could they do this   ?

They herd together
red collar, red letter
ovaryectomy
              why not castrate the bucks?
This is how they did it!
knowing they herd together
Kill the bucks, kill the does
        red collars, read letters
humiliate, track, 'other' then invent
This is how they did it!

Deer herd together
This will be remembered
long after the people
have forgotten

In the cells of the Earth
they huddle now together

She holds fallow memory
the last insult
fuck you to the deer
 the citizens who loved them
to Mother Earth.
        This will be remembered.

Big
red
tags,
collars
too
heavy.
Calluses,
blisters rub
Tags in our
ears big enough
for the rifleman's
sight to miss us.

#324

Red tags catch on
trees. Collars too big
for our long necks
puss grows with pain
in our wombs,
bellies. Some of
us die anyway.

January 31, 2008

    Then
  hunters
    came

                                         Metal
                                        hellbirds
                                        overhead

              800
             to 80
           All our
            males
             dead

                                She
                             hears us
                            she who
                             sent us
                         hears these
                              shots
                                too

   We sing
  our shrill
  death cry
   for them

                                           We sing
                                      our ghost
                                      dance for
                                     the fallen

Pt. Reyes Earth Voice

There is no reason for this.

This wild peninsula of sweetness
traveling along my coast
skating up
the thigh of my world,
will continue to
travel

long after humans
have
dissapeared.

"Deer carcasses are to be sent to
homeless shelters in large white boxes"[1]

Packing Slip:
Instructions: How to Tan a Deer Hide

To: St. Anthony Foundation
        150 Golden Gate Avenue
        San Francisco, CA 94102

From: White Buffalo Hunters,
NPS Pt. Reyes National Seashore,
Olema, CA 94956

Packing Slip Contents:
20 dead assorted deer - minus racks

Directions: Strip hide off
butcher carcass accordingly

Tanning instructions below:

Take one deer pelt
Scrape the fascia off the inside
Take the brains cook them
until just before they boil

If they burn you, they'll cook the hide.
Let them cool, then rub in vigorously,
Don't let the skin dry out, cover every inch,
the brains will soak in. Stretch on a rack to dry.

Uses: Skins provide warmth and protection:
good for moccasins, belts, shirts, traditional wedding dress.[2]

---

12. S.F. Chronicle Article, January 2008
13. From "Ghost of White Deer Story" – Chikasaw People - White Deer Hides are still prized for weddings as the deer and women are considered sacred.

No Middle Way - Pt. Reyes, CA, 2008

NPS hires White Buffalo Hunters
despite   protests,   letters from children,
Congresswomen, Senators   pleading manage
     these deer species
don't exterminate
all   to no   avail.

In 2007 through January 31, 2008,   NPS killed all
250 Axis deer   900 Fallow deer
80 females sterilized   remain

tagged with   red numbers   collars
with   tracking signals
         Before the killing, 1 per 30 acres
         after killing, 1 per 110 acres

      All 250 Axis deer (brown, black, yellow, white)
         Gone in just one killing spree
Vedanta Retreat, Olema, CA
               have sheltered deer
         are shocked at violence of program

       baiting, nets, high-powered weapons, netting,
stabbing, and plastic bags   used to kill deer.[1]

Corpses were air lifted to   homeless shelters
in huge   white boxes   after   this

     massacre   ! Some eye witnesses saw garbage truck
heading for landfills
         Collars were removed after   all   the males
were   dead.

---

14. San Francisco Chronicle, Friday April, 11, 2008

Afterwards   grief stricken residence

   of Pt. Reyes

constructed   a wailing wall.

Question #2 for the Shooter

How did you come to use the White Buffalo logo, and equate your company with the story of the Lakota woman, White Buffalo Calf Woman, the Native American saint, who first brought the sacred pipe for the people to live?

I was trying to convey how
interconnected to nature we are.
Having worked with suburban mentality
there is a huge disconnect with people
from their environment.   *(I will agree with you on this one.)*

I liked how Native people
believed they were tied to nature
                              *(They know they are part of,
                                embedded into nature)*
and how they managed their species   *(But wait, Native people
                                never managed their species,
                                they related to the animals*

they took as relatives, they gave thanks,
never assumed superiority,
they prayed for their survival, for the people,
all people, animal people, tree people, white people, brown and black
people, yellow people
for the survival of the Earth, for balance)

they are part of the environment   *(True)*
They add a human dimensional element. *(They know they are part of all life, Mother Earth, Father Sky, they know they are embedded into nature, not above it.)*
Native people get they were a part of it.   *(Yes)*
Most people, because of technology,
are so disconnected from it.   *(True)*

How do I live my life?   *(I can't imagine, how do you live with yourself)*
I try to live according to my values.   *(!#&*@!?*?)*
I clean up after other people. *(In your "clean up" did you ever once think about the emotional impact of your killing, or the spiritual, your karma, do you know about karma???)*
It's more a values thing. *(The value to kill whatever you want in the name of science? Where are you drawing your line in time?)*
I can't do anything without *(If I were Diana, I would turn you into Actaeon, so you could be your own prey.)*
other agencies intervening.
We can't have predators, *(People live within the wild all the time in the mountains, every neighbor lost a cat, or dog, to mountain lions, it was the price we paid for living with them so close.)*
bears kill people. *(So do humans. More humans kill people than bears!)*
We are more dominant, that is a fact.
(Validating your own tendencies, we have more, a lot more to us than predation. We become what we practice. That is a fact.)

Here it is.   Thank you for your interview.

What I want to say to you, hunter,
These birds and deer of all colors, these
squirrels are my relatives. They are
my family, even as a white woman,
educated, like you, how the buck
that was killed by you, with his big black
palmate antlers, was my father, his beard
blowing under in the fog wind. The doe
with white spots and tawny fur, my mother,
sister a piebald deer, daughter the fawn,
not pets, relatives. No, they don't match
my outer skin color, or species,
that doesn't matter. All I know is,
they only swim in a grief-river
towards me   in my sleep
night after
infinite
night.

Through trees we see breasts / the road where we stopped on our date / No stars but two through fog

This road leads to Olema &

Through the trees we see breasts of the mother

Glimpses / not a / owls shelters mice / below / the earth is showing / what are we doing? / peek / These oak houses / that dropped pellets / from mice where she rose up / see her lift to leaves

Glimpses through the trees how

Just another day / one I'll not forget / no I do not so infringe on the Glimpse of things / Rise up up to eat day leaves / There is where I saw her rising up here / to eat a leaf. / Down the road we saw them / taking this road to the bees / There they focused over mother / she

right Jon over here — / Trail It goes to the monks houses / where I saw / lamps + bare heads Then / No not that way — just this way / rocks over / spread all / spots on a mountain but so much more / I think I see her / take this / from here I see her / loop around Then down this path

Down and down / found a Bone here / Over this trail I see them or / Down the hill I see them or one

To find our lost deer

reach inside. Return to your own garden

Grief takes the time it takes

each in our own way.

The whole story is there   from all times.

It is   a trick a lie   a twist we bought.

Each one of us   is   recovering   the soul   of humanity,

listen. Release all fear. Nothing more to lose.

You stopped them, there are a few left.

This is some sort of victory.

What will

you do

to prevent a repeat

of history?

Gentle deer,   friends

        Our lost family,

Ones wandering

        on the hills,

not lost,
        though grazing

somewhere.

                              Deer

                               say

Sit still   and let the fawn   come to you

Let the brown   red   yellow   white

spotted   fawn

                            come.

Let it nuzzle   your   ear

Let it sniff   you   gently   and then

walk   on.

Let   this   fawn

                       be   born

in   you

                            again.

What These Deer Mean

They were a

Sign

that somewhere there are ears in the Universe listening

Proof

that innocence is carried on the backs of the meek

Evidence

of how cruel eradication of a invasive species is

Testimony,

these deer are a sign   proof   evidence

of

evaporation

of   a   sacred   wild   world

as it disappears.

Earth
    is so damaged
she keens   into the air
   saying: *This grief*
infuses my body from your ignore-ance

We already have   lost
   are loosing

    This is a love letter to her,
the screams are deafening
               if you are listening

  Creatures have other ways of being
       rather than ways of doing.   Are you
hearing anything yet ???   Feel.

maybe maybe not maybe maybe not   you will,
   maybe   you will
 maybe just maybe maybe just maybe
  you will   perhaps   no time left really
  no kidding   maybe you will maybe
                its past time   maybe just maybe
  Science reduces
     unless it observes with heart
  no heart
  no thing remains
 take nuclear waste, Fukishima, take all these random killings,
 take the slow poisonous death of millions to cancer these are signs

reductionism is killing us
  poisoning Earth is not an option anymore   There are consequences,
        what are the consequences?
     Elders say: take only what you need, then give back something
needed and desired by the Earth, give thanks for what you get,
gather around fires and hold a ceremony to say so.
 Feed the Earth with your prayers, with your love for her well being.

                Soon you will know.

Earth to Humans

My body Earth

contains a living being.

I will not ask for your love.

we have a relationship

regardless.

There are consequences to your blindness.

It has all been given, or taken, from me.

You have change in your veins you know,

your emotions change weather,

your heart beats with mine.

Your body is the Earth,

you poison yourselves.

I am not kidding.

She Called Herself
Black Hair Silk Girl Wind

Espero alegre la salida
y espero no volver jamás
last written words of Frida Kahlo

You were wrapped in plaster countless times,
spine   disintegrating   at the end
                        foot
            amputated, no other cage could remain so ignited
No moon, diamond, sun,   hands fingertip dot   gauze, sea pine green,

Cage of ribs and body broken in too many pieces
                    Body by the bus, heart by Diego
Cage of ribs by Diego, body by the bus
                        You called *Dove*   Diego *Toad*
he drew you a picture of a dove lighting on a toad.

            Dove, toad, mud, gangrene, sunflower, sinister blue,
illusive pillar, every moment he is my child,
        black hair silk girl wind, yellow love, child flower, article resin

deer shot with arrows, with Frida's face   falling
            Inside the arms of the Great Earth Mother,
                            holding Diego a baby,
painted your baby miscarried coming from your womb,
        transfusion tubes coming from your uterus to a floating world

death   a constant companion.   *I hope the leaving is joyful*
    May the curtain you walked through become water become salve,
                    become freedom,

May you exceed your dreams in the coming world
                        and I hope never to return

    May he love only you in your next incarnation
                        cage open to set dove free
        hollow bone song
                May you soar!

Piebald Deer

A white deer with brown spots came to me a piebald deer transfering from one world to the next - according to ledgend, piebald are spirits of dead returning. (lanape people)

My sister came to me the other day. She held my heart from behind me, as her spirit rose up leaning over she whispered, "You are so loved", over + over.

As I lay in bed trying to read, she held on gently until my chest was stitched and healed, until there was a scab + a large bandage no one could see but me & her. I rested in her arms.

My sister came to me, a piebald deer, pure & hopeful, a white deer with brown spots, as clear as the dots on my hands. Kisti dear, hovering around, reminding me, all things are healed with love.

Culling Continues

"Why do they have to hide it?"[1]

Walker, your footsteps are the road...

Hired hunters block off roads
from protestors to slaughter

Walker, there is no road

Shooters drive into the area on ATVs,
trucks or on foot.

there is no road made of walking

"They should just do it

walking you make the road

out in the open

and turning to look behind

if they believe

*you see the path
you will never again step upon.*

it is the right thing to do."

*Walker. there is no road,
only foam trails on the sea.*[2]

---

15. Exasperated C. Machado, Director Humane Society as she looks down from above at idle park rangers and White Buffalo Hunters ready for the kill. San Francisco Chronicle, Thursday, January 31, 2008.
16. *Italics: Antonio Machado untitled poem called "walker"*. Non-italicized: Quoting Cynthia Machado, Director of Humane Society found language from San Francisco Chronicle, Thursday, January 31, 2008

Everything without tags and a collar
will be shot. [1]

A pigeon green and pink on its poking neck
in out in out grey in shades
everywhere else.

Three female ducks two males ones
mallards one a green head,
extravagant bird the other purple-headed
a black and purple duck come up to a woman
in the park near the pond

Everyday black-footed birds swim poke around breed.
A mountain and bay away deer roam
hillsides grazing drinking from streams
Their tags and collars suppose to protect them
too big, the wrong size
chafing.

---

17. Headline, SF Chronicle, January 31st, 2008

Gon-a-con Blues
"It's so unnecessary"[1]

Ranchers,
finding deer carcasses
on trails near residences
put residence
and park visitors
at risk,
ask for moratorium.

White buffalo hunters use
Helicopters to drive them out
in the open,
80 does captured
surgically sterilizing
shoot remaining males
inject female deer
with Gon-a-con Blue.
Wildlife eugenics,
Tuskeegee-like experiments
cause baseball sized
abscesses.

This is known before
the hunt.
Even after
Boxer and Feinstein
wrote letter for
non-lethal methods.

After petitions against slaughter
asking for non-lethal methods,
infuriated politicians,
animal rights activists,
environmentalists,
Gon-a-con Blue was used.
Until NPS pulled funding,
bowing to political
pressure, $750,000 later

Red taged females
left with red collars as a
red letter 'A' on body of females,
wasn't this done before?
Can we ask ourselves
Are we improving?
Just yokes, no stocks?

18. San Francisco Chronicle, Thursday, January 31, 2008C. Machado, Director Marin Humane Society

Plan #1

Sneak in after dark
Become a monk
Become a hermit so they
don't notice me

Bathe first and approach
down wind
wear camo

Cut those tags
off. Remove the collar carefully.

Pet the deer gently, as she lay
sleeping in the grass.

Plan #2

Shoot the Superintendent
with a sleeping dart

Pierce his ears with big holes
place tags removed from deer

in his ears while
sleeping

cinch the red collar tight
lock it in the back where he

can't reach upon waking
leave a note:

Now you are
314.

After the Kill[1]

Native deer
lay at trailhead
in fields
dying.

Every day more deer
appear to be
dying

Parasitic
worms
consuming deer
organs
as they lay
dying

Axis
and Fallow deer
have a natural resistance
to worms
having evolved
in warmer climates

No deer will be left
Tourists and residence fear
Is this the result of the kill?
Something is dying

Park chief scurries to find
surplus Fallow deer
cheap,
to replace
native deer
that lay dying.

---

19. Point Reyes Light, February 28, 2008, Letter to editor by Diane Alders, Bolinas, CA.

The Search

Spanish moss drips off trees
spills green softness in long grasses
Wrens move in and out of tree limbs
where they nest in low bent branches
four-hundred feet away from Vendanta Center's gate
beneath a huge oak I sit and wait
for the monk in the truck to leave

If I sit very still will their ghosts come to visit?
These white deer, aberrations,
native people would say what is of white
fur holds more light, deflects what is not.

Watch the truck and the man in a veil
collecting honey from bees,
as he checks the hives then drives further away.
If the tap, tap valve of that truck goes over the hill it climbs
if I light across this field in my blue shirt and straw hat
will I be disguised enough in sky
clouds, branches, wind   tap, tap this freight train
of the truck engine
will I see a herd or one or two?

Up that hill to find them, up and up, scan the wilderness.
look for my friends under trees,
ducking bending low a trail winds past the oak
a well worn mowed trail. It winds over road, paved black top scars,
the hill's slow ascent. Up half way
off the trail a bench, place to look back, over browning thighs of hills
those dark green triangles of trees settle in low rivulets.
Earth is a woman from here, sitting a moment, scrying
the hills—no sign of deer—after the massacre—a few left I heard
trails wind up and up, a snake trail where
fox glove, small five petals, pink and white blessings,
ferns, redwoods, bay, thick forest trail winds through
them, along way up and up
as path becomes a clearing
grass spotlights of sun blue patches against green

no one but me, no deer, though scat
of coyote and oh deer you have been here!
Something standing peed something long enough to leave
a fresh mark on the trail less than an hour old
not a man nor a woman. A four legged,
a penis underneath a long body
further up the hill and further still
until an invisible hand on my back says turn back.
Too late, too far along in the day to go much further,
on the ridge now, woods shrouded
I turn around, back down the field
in the clearings with veils of light falling
Orixa holy elements
Jerema, light of the forest,
with her lover Oxassi, the hunter,
like Daphne and Cloe, he
chases after her never catches her
here and there in the glade
these patches where we could lay
bright spots where they turn into
memory of light they chase then linger as
I seek the golden moment, that illusive day,
when I see them once again.
There are no deer now, not white
nor red, not black, nor yellow.
Their floating gate, their gentleness escapes me,
where Jurema and Oxassi are running around
making love then fleeing each other,
the hunter and his lover
down through the green of sun and dark shadows
Down through trees and woods and flowers
stopping to survey the ocher fields below
nothing on nothing, I surrender, oh perhaps,
those deer have to want to be seen.
It is afternoon, after all, before their dinnertime perhaps.

A long way down the hill,
one last survey of pubic hair trees
and brown ridges under an oak arbor, I spot
a white shape, a star as it moves,

make out the shape of the tree
and in its shadow
it is playing I see it,
turning, raising up into branches
bending down, hunching it's back.
It is a white deer moving bright in shadow
I snap a picture so far away
too far away to get a clear shot.
Keeping my eye on the tree and shadow that shape
winding down through
grasses thigh high the sun
after shadowed trees is
bright white spot moving
then gone.

Remembering my shades left under the great oak
I spot the tree on my way down and there in the grass
at my feet, a shoulder blade. It's a
deer blade white with two round holes
—pellet shaped holes—
too round to have been anything but made by bullets. Evidence
of the shootings on peaceful Vedanta ground.
This bone is a gift I decide.
Leave my white hair, find my shades
in the shade under the oak,
move towards another tree bending
over trail deeper shadows as the sunlight grows angled
where the rest of them fell right here in this field,
fell into the shadows of trees
where they fell into oblivion   too deep for them
where now fresh scat is there on the trail
right there where I saw one raise up to nibble
branches minutes ago and here
deer pellets and near by a bit down the trail,
a place where one slept
just one,
What would it be like to be the last?

As Ishi, a Yahi, the last California wild Indian, [1]
how lonely he was

how lonely this she-deer must be,
How is it we have come to this,
killing off the rare whether deer or a human being?

I saw one just now, have evidence of a shoulder blade,
take home an owl feather
not far from the scat left and owl pellets of packed
mouse fur and bone bits, compacted regurgitations
at owl's favorite dinner place, a hole in the ground.

Ishi would say owl is death, as many who love the wild know
with silent wings, opens doors we fall through.
I move down and down some more
towards dinner, after all afternoon
I have searched for you,
a grateful moment of contact
where a single white deer,
at least one lone female,
I know still roams.

20.. Ishi: The Last of his Tribe, with Eloy Casados in the title role, telecast on NBC, December 20, 1978, a film written by Christopher Trumbo.

Necessary Elegance - How to view this single reminent scientifically Detachment is... part of Descartian thinking, take only the body

This is the end of joint of scapula or nipptions of shoulder and scapula - Slightly convex to articulate with socket of shoulder.

Fallow deer shoulder

bump

Profile of Ridge - Trace the lines of bones and you see how they functioned

If you see the sinew and ligaments attach on all sides - joint-like-force, sharpness muscles and bone do not make the animal - spirit, life force, shapes protects the heart from the back and others a place for attachments the deer must run away from danger.

found on trail after seeing a white deer — fallow — Tallow — Built for

attached on either side of this bony ridge

How the flesh has been eaten. How the muscle would have

Contours are lovely

The two are not contradictory

"built hole"

Bones form foundational structures — incredible, necessary elegance grace, long linear curves.

of predator? Pare - size - or built hole

Bright Sighting, 2011

        Through the trees see the green breasts of
                breasts of our mother

A glimpse, just a peek, through the trees   bright sighting

One not to forget, hunting for her
she might be the last one
over here
      Not this trail - It goes to the monk's house - lamps and bare heads
                          in windows

No not that way   where the yellow truck is gathering honey
                          from bees

See the shapes of trails   how
                  the Earth is turning
Hunting for the last of a breed
                  Here is a sign
         The oaks house owls, shelters mice below
             Owls drop pellets
       From eating mice where she rose up
              Is that one?
Take this route   - see her?

Down this road   witness
       Take this road to the bees- turn left then right
                    zig and
zag down
                this steep hill

Brown fecund Earth perceive   those spots on the mountain?
                Are they living things?

Perhaps it is   them   remains of a herd

                         This path
                  Found a deer shoulder blade here
           Where none were to be killed, did it die of old age? Holes in it
                         Could be bullet holes
Over this trail   glimpse
                       Down the hill see one,
                         Lifting to leaves

One   just   one

                           left.

Dream for Deer

Save one in tack, or two
set them free somewhere
else put them in an ark

Return them to reserves
in Iran or Iraq
where they came from

In Pt. Reyes, hope the NPS missed killing a few
males missed sterilizing a few more females
so they return

No more collateral damage to a murdering mentality

But instead considered just a pest, not like *our own* black-tailed deer,
white, or brown, or tawny, or black
now these deer, after the fact are declared a national treasure.

When you get too rare or common, too many, too happy, to showy, too much, too flamboyant too,

too two just two too   label invasive and kill or endangered save one please

killing is justified, exterminate them, too, too,   too two   just
too by two

Noah where are you?

like a mosquito, swat,   pow   bang,   by NPS

Death of the Wild

So many species disappearing
        Wild Horses in Wyoming
        Condors in California
Fallow Deer and Axis deer in Iraq and Iran
        and in Marin County, California

When the wild goes our own wild is lost
For what?   *Green frog skins*   my Lakota teacher, Buck,
                used to say,
        not even backed with gold anymore!

Going deep in your verticality below where your feet
        touch into Earth
                repair the bites of your grounding cord by loving it

the wild is
        bring it into your cage of ribs

    when we love our own
    wolves and wolverines
    bats and rattlesnakes
    mountain lions, and jaguars
    grizzly bears and white deer

Then we will love the wild
and all our awkward moments

we will slow down cattle grazing taking wild lands
        and stop eating so much beef.

        for Kate and the newTribe

Along mountain base
light on
willow strands
lilac bush
oak –
a million green
coins

ducks are swimming
sun streaks my face
and warms it.

Nature
simply
matters.

Mountain my bread
fly my humm
light
on leaves on ducks
swim through this
presence,

a calm of place
of deer grazing
the river
this circle of
fog
lifting.

After the
massacre
some
deer
were seen
in the sky
joining
the Milky Way.

Some
entered
their
hunters
bodies.
Lives
shortened.
Lives taken
in restitution.

So say the
Lanapé
people.[1]

---

21. *Llewellyn's Magic Almanac: Practical Magic for Everyday Living*, Elizabeth Barrette, Llewellyn's Deborah Blake, Ellen Dugan, Llewellyn Publishers, St. Paul, Minn., p. 130

The deer on this canvas

appear when I look at those green winter hills

soon to be painted midnight blue. Brush marks will be thick

and their seven bodies will be floating away.

Though as I paint them, I know hardly any

are still alive today to wander as they once

did foraging on the next ridge.

Now,

in my painting to honor them

these seven white deer

graze on a billion stars.

Lament for the Deer People

Shining in the inky firmament
no longer the deer-child
once carried
no longer a womb-bound
earth-tied star,
no longer here.

You were once a dream
a living moon
a sea of white deer
pouring over dark hillsides

Moon of glowing sky
fallen over fields and green hills
a river-herd
of blue bones
a tide given back
to the turquoise sea
always shining beyond
the storm ruined sky.

for Mar-i-Luna del Sol

Full moon
clock tower striking nine
ghost deer pour forth
from white disk
into a silver
oval field

one-thousand and fifty
stand around
with all of us
who love them
still

They come
back
to softly
nuzzle us and say

thank you
for loving us
so well

We
forgive

Just know
love
is all
that
remains

Acknowledgements

There are many people I wish to thank. First of all, my professors from Mills College, Stephen Ratcliffe, and Juliana Spahr, as well as Truong Tran, Patricia Powell, and Ruth Saxon. Stephen and Juliana were primary mentors as well as the students in my graduate program in poetry who supported this work with critical eyes and open hearts including Linda King, Claudia Heron, Penina Tesali, Janelle Hayward, Kate Mensies, Kat Howard, Kate Robinson, Emji Spero, Brittany Billomeyer-Finn, Cheena Marie Lo, Brian Roth, and many others. Also thank you to Professor Huma Dar who first introduced me to Agha Shahed Ali's work, and who provide much information on Persian poetry.

Many thanks to the people in west Marin County, California, especially Tess Elliot, editor of the Point Reyes Light, who provided me with stacks of articles on the deer, and the people who wrote them, both pro and con. Many of the main protestors and organizers including Kathy Runion, Christine DeCamp, David Mitchell, Ella Walker, Richard Hirschman, Doris Ober, and Friends of the White Deer who provided a book of letters, articles, photographs, posters, and information about the deer from the several newspapers including the Marin Independent Journal, The San Francisco Chronicle, and the Pt. Reyes Light. Thanks also to the president of White Buffalo, Inc. Anthony DeNicola, the hunter who agreed to be interviewed by phone. Don Neubacher the Superintendent of Pt.Reyes National Seashore who was the primary target of much of the criticism and without whom, this book and much of the rhetoric around the incidents of 2007-08 would not have been written about nor deer mourned. I do not thank him in any way for his blindness, total inflexability, nor his lack of compassion for the people of Marin County and the deer. I also thank friend Todd Barto, and others who worked nearby, the NPS website, White Buffalo website, White Deer of Marin Website, and many web sources listed in the back of the book.

I would also like to thank my teachers in the Lakota Tradition, the late Buck Ghost Horse, Paul and Inez Ghost Horse, Vicki Ghost Horse, and many friends and extended family in the Sinte Gleshka Oyate, especially Blake and Veronica Basham, Steve and Lori Coyote, Judy Shaffer, Dana Jain who gave me on going feedback, and Jenni, Kirin Jain, my nieces with whom I traveled back and forth to ceremony. My friends Barbara Amita, Sherrie Dorr, who provided tremendous support and feedback, and Linda King at Mills who offered a perspective I appreciated. I would also like to thank my friends on Rosebud Indian Reservation,

Florentine Blue Thunder and the Blue Thunder family who opened their hearts to us who were drawn to the Lakota ways and teachings. Thank you to my poetry critique group, Emerald Street poets, as they reviewed some of thise poems. Thanks also to Cecil S. Giscombe who helped through our conversations through the summer of 2011 about poetry, and who provided a catalyzing effect on my work.

Last but never least, my late father Robert E. Heerens, who passed at age 99 who provided unwavering belief in my right and need to do a program that seems impractical, and my sisters, nieces and nephews who, in their own ways, offered familial support through their on-going cheerleading.

Finally, I would like to thank the deer, and the Mother Earth who feels all, knows all and sees what we are doing, and for whom I dedicate this work.

Mitake Oyasin (for all my relations),

        Robin White Turtle Lysne, M.F.A., Ph.D.

List of Sources

Friends of the White Deer of Marin County website:

    www.friendsofthewhitedeer.org

Gerrard, Greg, *Ecocriticism, The New Critical Idiom*, Routledge, New York, NY, 2004

Ghost of the White Deer Story - Chikasaw People, archiver.rootsweb.ancestry.com/th/read CHEROKEE/...1140568954

Ishi: The Last of his Tribe, with Eloy Casados in the title role, telecast on NBC, December 20, 1978, a film written by Christopher Trumbo.

Llewellyn's Magic Almanac: Practical Magic for Everyday Living, Elizabeth Barrette, Llewellyn's Deborah Blake, Ellen Dugan, Llewellyn Publishers, St. Paul, Minn., p. 130

Marin Independent Journal, San Rafael, CA

National park Service website: www.nps.gov

Point Reyes Light, Olema, CA

San Francisco Chronicle, San Francisco, CA

Pt. Reyes National Seashore website: www.nps.gov/pore/

White Buffalo Incorporated website: www.whitebuffaloinc.org

About the Author

Robin White Turtle Lysne was born in Rockford, Illinois and has lived in California since 1987. She is the author of four books of nonfiction. *Dancing Up The Moon, Sacred Living*, (both Conari Press, Berkeley, CA), *Heart Path, Learning to Love Yourself and Listening to Your Guides*, (Blue Bone Books, Santa Cruz, CA), and *Heart Path Handbook, An Energy Medicine Guide*, for therapists and healers. She also has a new series of books called Legendary Ancestor Women Series. Though she has written many poems for her non-fiction books, and had others published over the years, *Poems for the Lost Deer* is her first book of poems published in a single volume. Her poems have been published in *Sand Canyon Review, North American Review, Samizdat Literary Journal, Porcupine Literary Arts Magazine, Awaken Consciousness Magazine, Santa Cruz Weekly,* and other periodicals, and in *Harvest from the Emerald Orchard* and other anthologies. She has been featured reader at Poetry Express in Berkeley, Writing without Walls and the Samizdat Literary Journal release reading in San Francisco, and Poet/Speak in Santa Cruz, CA. Her poem "First Step" was selected for reading by survivors at the Virginia Tech Memorial Bench Dedication in 2010. Her art work has been shown widely in the Midwest and on the East Coast. She received her MFA from Mills College in 2012 and her PhD in Energy Medicine in 2013 from the University of Natural Medicine, Santa Fe, NM. She is a owner/publisher of Blue Bone Books. (BBB poetry is a cooperative press) and a professional Psychic/Medium and Energy Medicine Practitioner through out the San Francisco Bay Area and across the country by phone. Her websites are: www.thecenterforthesoul.com, www.bluebonebooks.com, and or www.robinlysne.com.

What other say about Poems for the Lost Deer:

Poems for the Lost Deer is much more than poems. It is a tract that is, at once, lamentation and praise song, dirge and testament and manifestation. And an inquiry into values and hierarchy and a series of addresses to the faces of power. At stake is the extermination of the white deer of Marin County—"culling" is the word, the "Management Plan." We need be mindful of St. George: "Such phraseology is needed if one wants to name things without calling up mental pictures of them." But it's also the gap, it's that Wordsworth's "Where I could meditate in peace, and cull/ Knowledge that step by step might lead me on/ To wisdom…." gives way to—as Lysne reports in these pages—"Culling/ Education/ Garbage cans." *Poems for the Lost Deer* invites readers to try to comprehend the scope and scale of the hillsides and of "what humans do."
—C. S. Giscombe (author of *Into & Out of Dislocation*, etc.)

Echoing Blake's Songs of Innocence and Experience, Robin Lysne's Poems for the Lost Deer documents the recent systematic slaughter of "non-native" Axis and Fallow deer from the Point Reyes National Seashore. Presenting "what happened" in an assemblage of overlapping voices -- factual "evidence". "In 2007 through January 31, 2008, NPS killed all / 250 Axis deer 900 Fallow deer / Before the killing, 1 per 30 acres / after killing, 1 per 110 acres / All 250 Axis deer (brown, black, yellow, white) / Gone in just one killing spree."; the National Park Service "Pick a date, draw a line. // Whatever team of experts deemñ / this is the way isî); those who did the shooting "We are more dominant, that is a fact."; those who protested it ("Who are not labeled an invasive species?"); those who took care of the remains ("Deer carcasses are to be sent to / homeless shelters in large white boxes"// "Packing Slip Contents: / 20 dead assorted deer ñ minus racks"); and throughout it all the deer themselves -- first innocent ("Across this / field an apple tree / full of blossoms / run to it, sniff / stretching our necks / rub antlers on bark / scratch ears with hooves, / nuzzle young / we live / one more spring") then experienced ("Humans came / to stop the / hunters // They gave us / three more suns / before the massacre") and now forever gone ("thank you / for loving us / so well // We / forgive // Just know / love / is all / that / remains". This is a glimpse of the book Robin Lysne has given us, one whose time has come not a moment too soon.

Stephen Ratcliffe. Author of *Real, Portraits and Repitition, and over 20 books of poetry and criticism, and is a long time Professor at Mills College.*

This manuscript is passionate, compassionate, skillful, meticulous, graceful, vital, and heartbreaking. It's most powerful moments lie in the poems that allow readers to come to their own conclusion and make their own connections, without being told exactly what to think. A shining moment lies in "Question #1 for the Shooter," which demonstrates a disturbing mentality "the nonchalant attitude of a niche I fell into" and the strange idea that "You can't think about the/individual animal." This type of heartlessness as revealed in the language of the manuscript's antagonists also seen in poems like "The Politics of Shooting Deer" and "Question #3 for a Park Ranger" is juxtaposed beautifully, albeit sorrowfully, with the poet's own outpourings of lyrical emotion and compassion for the deer, as in gems like "Down there comes a fallow Doe" and "They herd together." The use of repetition, refrain, found language through extensive research, and a variety of poem types all weave together elegantly.

Heather Nagami, Editor of Overhere Press, Professor Northeastern University, Boston.

This engaged and engaging sequence of poems by Robin Lysne sees permeable borders where others see boundaries.; it is a kind of wordsmithery that is at once committed to changing our given worlds and to imagining spiritual worlds we have not yet reached.

Though the subject is ostensibly the historical destruction of te white deer at Pt. Reyes peninsula between 2007-8, the reach is broader. When a voice speaks from one of the poems to say: "We sing/our ghost/dance for/the fallen," deer and native and poet sing together of the past to question our future.

Through drawings, prose fragments, and lyrics, the poet deals in weighty matters, but with a deft touch that always allows the mysteries of nature to seep in and color everything. Let us listen hard to her singing.

David Allen Sullivan, Professor Cabrillo College, Author of Strong-Armed Angels, Every Seed of the Pomegranate.

www.ingramcontent.com/pod-product-compliance
Lightning Source LLC
Chambersburg PA
CBHW072057290426
44110CB00014B/1716